Ultimate Travel Guide To

Trondheim, NORWAY

*Traveling to Trondheim?
Don't Leave Home Without This Guide!*

Elizabeth Whyte

Table of Contents

COPYRIGHT NOTICE

This publication is copyright protected. This is only for personal use. No part of this publication may be, including but not limited to, reproduced, in any form or medium, stored in a data retrieval system or transmitted by or through any means, without prior written permission from the Author / Publisher.

Legal action will be pursued if this is breached.

SCAN TO SEE ALL MY BOOKS

DISCLAIMER

Please note that the information contained within this document is for educational purposes only. The information contained herein has been obtained from sources believed to be reliable at the time of publication. The opinions expressed herein are subject to change without notice.

Readers acknowledge that the Author / Publisher is not engaging in rendering legal, financial or professional advice. The Publisher / Author disclaims all warranties as to the accuracy, completeness, or adequacy of such information.

The Publisher assumes no liability for errors, omissions, or inadequacies in the information contained herein or from the interpretations thereof. The publisher / Author specifically disclaims any liability from the use or application of the information contained herein or from the interpretations thereof.

TABLE OF CONTENT

Copyright Notice
Disclaimer
Table of Content
Introduction
Welcome To Trondheim, Norway!

- About This Travel Guide
- How to Use This Guide
- Trondheim Travel Tips

Chapter 1
Getting Acquainted with Trondheim

- Trondheim in a Nutshell
- Trondheim's Historical Background
- Climate and Geography
- Traditions and Culture in Trondheim
- Local Expressions and Phrases

Chapter 2
Planning Your Trip

- When to Go to Trondheim
- Entry Requirements and Visas
- Budgeting for Your Trip
- Accommodation Options
- Transportation to Trondheim
- Conclusion

Table of Contents

Chapter 3
Trondheim Exploration

    Neighborhoods and City Planning

    Landmarks and Attractions Not to Miss

    Galleries and museums

    Parks and Outdoor Recreation

    Trondheim Shopping

Chapter 4
Experiencing Trondheim's Culinary Delights

    Norwegian Cuisine at its Finest

    Seafood Specialties

    Restaurants, Cafes, and Bars

    Markets and Street Food

    Dietary Options and Restrictions

Chapter 5
Participating in Local Activities

    Hiking and Other outdoor Activities

    Winter Recreation

    Festivals and Special Events

    Entertainment and Nightlife

    Wellness and relaxation

Chapter 6
Getting Around Trondheim

    Public Transportation

    Renting a Vehicle

Table of Contents

    Bike Riding in Trondheim

    Taxis and Ride-Sharing Services

    Accessibility in Trondheim

Chapter 7
Day Trips and Excursions

    Tours of Coastal Villages and Fjords

    Trondheim's Surrounding Natural Beauty

    Historical and Cultural Day Trips

    Adventure and Wildlife Excursions

    Planning Your Day Trips

Chapter 8
Interacting with Locals

    Social Protocol and Customs

    Friendship in Trondheim

    Sustainable and Responsible Tourism

    How to Stay Safe in Trondheim

    Emergency Information

Chapter 9
Travel Resources

    Tourist Information Centers

    Consulates and Embassies

    Communication and the Internet

    Money Matters

    Travel Insurance

Chapter 10

Table of Contents

Appendix
- Sample Itineraries
- Packing List for Trondheim
- Useful Norwegian Expressions
- Additional Reading and References

Introduction

WELCOME TO TRONDHEIM, NORWAY!

Trondheim, a city as gorgeous as it is historically rich. I can still recall my first visit to this charming Norwegian gem. Frankly, I can't wait to share my insights and recommendations with you in this travel guide.

About This Travel Guide

This book is the result of my own travel through Trondheim, which was full of experiences and discoveries.

It's supposed to be your faithful buddy while you explore this lovely city. You'll find something here to fit your interests, whether you're a history buff, a foodie, an outdoor enthusiast, or all of the above.

I've written this guide to be as informative as possible, including suggestions for activities, restaurants, and cultural insights.

While I've covered the essentials, keep in mind that Trondheim, like any other city, is always changing. So, be open to venturing beyond the pages of the guide and generating your own unique experiences.

How to Use This Guide

The guide is simple to follow! You can begin at the beginning or skip ahead to the areas that interest you. Here's a basic rundown of how it works:

Getting Acquainted with Trondheim:

Learn about the city's history, culture, and geography. Discover what makes Trondheim distinctive.

Planning Your Trip:

Discover the best time to travel, visa requirements, financial advice, and how to get to Trondheim.

Exploring Trondheim:

Explore Trondheim's neighborhoods, must-see attractions, museums, parks, and retail areas.

Trondheim's Culinary Delights:

Savour the flavors of traditional Norwegian cuisine, seafood delicacies, and discover the best dining locations.

Participating in Local Activities:

Learn about hiking, outdoor excursions, festivals, and the bustling nightlife of the city.

Getting Around Trondheim:

Learn about public transportation, vehicle rentals, biking, and other practical information.

Excursions and Day Trips:

Plan your trips to seaside communities, fjords, and the surrounding natural beauties.

Interacting with Locals:

Discover local cultures, make new friends, practice responsible travel, and stay safe.

Travel Resources:

Learn about tourist attractions, embassies, communication, money, and insurance.

Appendix:

Discover sample itineraries, a packing list, useful Norwegian words, and a list of recommended reading in the appendix.

Trondheim Travel Tips

Now, let me give some helpful hints for making your trip to Trondheim an amazing experience:

1. Dress for the Weather:

Trondheim has a distinct climate, so bring layers and waterproof gear. Even in the summer, it's a good idea to keep a light jacket on hand.

2. Learn a Bit of Norwegian:

While many people in Trondheim speak English, locals appreciate it when you make an attempt to speak a few Norwegian words. A simple "takk" (thank you) can mean a lot.

3. Experience the Midnight Sun (or Northern Lights):

Depending on the season, you will either see the Midnight Sun or the stunning Northern Lights. Make your plans appropriately!

4. Respect the Natural Beauty:

Norway values its natural environment. Remember to leave no trace when exploring the outdoors - take your garbage with you and stick to specified trails.

5. Taste the Local Cuisine:

Don't leave Trondheim without sampling some authentic Norwegian cuisine. Enjoy a platter of

Raspeballer (potato dumplings) or some delectable lutefisk (lye-soaked dried fish).

6. Cash Isn't King:

Norway is largely cashless. Because credit and debit cards are generally accepted, you won't need to carry much cash.

7. Explore the Fjords:

Trondheim's proximity to the fjords is one of its most breathtaking features. To really enjoy their grandeur, take a fjord cruise or a day excursion.

8. Engage in Local Culture:

Interact with locals at festivals, markets, or community activities. This is where you can truly experience the soul of the city.

9. Embrace the Outdoors:

Whether you enjoy hiking, skiing, or simply meandering through gorgeous parks, Trondheim has it all. Pack your favorite pair of sneakers and get ready to explore.

10.   Finally, don't be afraid to become lost in the city's picturesque streets.

Some of my best discoveries in Trondheim occurred when I ventured off the beaten path.

Trondheim will steal your heart with its beauty, history, and inviting atmosphere. I hope you fall in love with this city as you read through this book and go on your adventure as I did.

Have a wonderful voyage filled with great moments and incredible adventures. Trondheim, cheers!

Chapter 1

GETTING ACQUAINTED WITH TRONDHEIM

Good day, fellow traveler! I'm very happy to share my adventures and experiences from my stay in Trondheim, Norway.

If you're thinking about visiting or just want to learn more about this wonderful city, this chapter is a great place to start.

Trondheim in a Nutshell

Trondheim is a picture-perfect postcard come to life. This city on the central Norwegian coast is known as the "Gateway to the North" because of its rich history and strategic location.

Trondheim offers a blend of modern living and ancient beauty, with its bustling streets, gorgeous buildings, and a touch of old-world charm.

Because of its small size, the city is ideal for touring on foot.

As you walk through its charming neighborhoods, you'll discover a city that perfectly blends the past with the contemporary. Cobblestone streets wind through old districts, while modern boutiques and cafes provide a sense of modern Norwegian life.

Trondheim's Historical Background

Trondheim's history reads like a captivating novel. In 997 AD, Viking King Olav Tryggvason founded Nidaros. It later became Norway's capital and an important center for medieval pilgrimage.

The majestic Nidaros Cathedral, a local landmark, stands as a witness to this historical significance.

Norway's constitution was signed here in 1814, paving the foundation for the contemporary Norwegian state. Trondheim's history is inextricably linked to the nation's identity, and you may learn about it in museums, historic places, and even by walking through its ancient streets.

Climate and Geography

Natural beauty surrounds Trondheim. The city is located beside the Trondheim Fjord, which provides breathtaking views of the water and green scenery. If you enjoy nature, there are several opportunities for hiking, skiing, and exploring the Norwegian wilderness just a short distance from the city.

Let us now talk about the climate.

Trondheim's winters may be bitterly cold, with plenty of snowfall, making it a popular location for winter sports aficionados. Summer, on the other hand, delivers the legendary Midnight Sun, when the sun never sets, resulting in lengthy, sun-drenched days. Spring and autumn have better weather, making them ideal for exploring the city and its environs.

Traditions and Culture in Trondheim

Trondheim is a city that values its heritage. Throughout the year, Norwegians celebrate a variety of festivals and cultural events. Christmas in Trondheim is especially magical, with the entire city illuminated with colorful lights and marketplaces selling homemade goods and local foods. Visit in May for National Day (17th of May) to see parades, traditional costumes, and spirited celebrations for a taste of Norwegian culture.

There is also a strong maritime culture in Trondheim, which is home to the Norwegian University of Science and Technology and other important research organizations. The fishing industry and the various seafood eateries dispersed across the city reflect the city's maritime influence.

Local Expressions and Phrases

While many Norwegians speak English fluently, it is always appreciated when visitors make an effort to learn a few Norwegian words. To help you get started, here are some simple phrases:

- "Hei" (Hi) - A friendly greeting.

- "Takk" (Thank you) - A simple way to express gratitude.
- "Unnskyld" (Excuse me/Sorry) - Useful in various situations.
- "Hvor er...?" (Where is...?) - Handy for asking for directions.
- "Kan jeg få...?" (Can I have...?) - Useful when ordering in a restaurant.

Engaging with residents in their original language can result in meaningful conversations and a more welcoming environment. So don't be afraid to give it a shot!

That concludes our first chapter on getting to know Trondheim. The city's rich history, magnificent geography, and dynamic culture make it a must-see.

As you read on, you'll learn about the best ways to explore Trondheim, from its attractions to its gastronomic delights and outdoor excursions. Stay tuned for more insights and recommendations to make your trip to Trondheim special!

Chapter 2

PLANNING YOUR TRIP

Hello once more, fellow explorers! In this chapter, I'll walk you through the details of planning your trip to Trondheim, Norway.

I've got you covered on everything from the ideal times to visit to entry criteria, budgeting, lodging, and transportation.

When to Go to Trondheim

When it comes to vacation planning, time is everything. Your experience in Trondheim will vary dramatically depending on the season.

Let's dissect it:

Summer (June to August): If you want long, sunny days and milder temperatures, summer is the best time to visit.

The legendary Midnight Sun, where the sun barely sets, provides plenty of daylight for exploration. This is when the city comes alive, with outdoor events, festivals, and a thriving street life. Simply expect increased costs and more tourists.

Autumn (September to November): Fall is a more peaceful and cost-effective time to visit. The temperature begins to cool, and the colors of the leaves in the neighboring forests are breathtaking. If you enjoy trekking and exploring without crowds, this is the season for you.

Snow (December to February): This is the jackpot for snow sports fans. Trondheim transforms into a snowy wonderland, with options for skiing, snowboarding, and ice skating.

Prepare for cold weather, but don't worry; Norwegians know how to keep warm and cozy.

Spring (March to May): As the snow melts, the city starts to defrost. Spring is ideal for individuals who want to witness the seasons change.

The days lengthen, and you may even see the Northern Lights. Remember that spring can be unexpected, so dress accordingly.

Entry Requirements and Visas

Before you pack your bags, be sure you have all of the appropriate travel paperwork. The good news is that most visitors to Norway will not require a visa for a short visit, especially if they are from a country in the European Union or the Schengen Area.

However, it's always a good idea to check with the Norwegian embassy or consulate in your home country for the most up-to-date admission procedures.

Check that your passport is valid for at least six months after your intended travel date. Always bring travel insurance that covers medical emergencies and trip cancellations. Although Norway is famed for having superb healthcare, you can never be too cautious.

Budgeting for Your Trip

Norway has a reputation for being somewhat pricey, so budgeting is an important element of vacation planning. Here are some price factors to consider:

Accommodation:

Accommodation in Trondheim can range from inexpensive hostels to luxury hotels, depending on your tastes.

On average, you can expect to pay between 900 and 2,500 NOK per night. Booking ahead of time or using Airbnb might occasionally save you money.

Food:

Dining out in Norway, particularly in restaurants, can be expensive. A simple lunch will cost roughly 150 NOK, whereas a three-course meal in a mid-range restaurant will cost 600 NOK or more.

You can, however, save money by eating at local cafes or enjoying some street food.

Activities: Many of Trondheim's attractions are free or have a minimal admission price. Museum tours and such things should cost roughly 100 NOK.

Don't forget to budget for day trips or excursions, such as fjord tours.

Transit: Public transit is convenient but expensive. A single bus or tram ticket costs about 36 NOK.

If you intend to visit surrounding cities or areas, the Norway in a Nutshell pass or other regional passes may be of interest.

Accommodation Options

Trondheim has a variety of lodging alternatives to suit a variety of budgets and interests. Here are a few popular options:

Hotels: Trondheim has a wide choice of hotels, from luxury to mid-range. Many of the options can be found in the city center.

Consider staying at a historic hotel with old-world elegance for a more distinctive experience.

Hostels: If you're on a budget, hostels are an excellent option. They provide a friendly environment and are ideal for meeting other travelers. Prices are lower when compared to hotels.

Airbnb: Renting an apartment or a room on Airbnb is a great way to immerse yourself in local culture. It's also a fantastic alternative for individuals looking for less expensive lodging.

Cabins and Cottages: Renting a cabin or cottage in the nearby countryside or near the fjords might be a terrific way to get closer to nature. It's perfect if you intend to spend a lot of time outside.

Transportation to Trondheim

Trondheim is relatively easy to reach thanks to well-connected transportation networks. Here are some options:

By Air: Trondheim Airport Vaernes (TRD) is the city's principal international gateway. It serves domestic and European flights, making it accessible to the majority of passengers. When you arrive, you can take an airport shuttle bus or a taxi to the city center.

By Train: If you're already in Europe, a gorgeous train excursion to Trondheim is an option. Norway's train system provides comfortable and scenic journeys from places such as Oslo and Bergen. Trondheim's train station is well positioned.

By Car: If you prefer to go by car, Trondheim is easily accessible thanks to Norway's well-maintained road network. Keep in mind that some regions may need a toll payment, and that winter tires and snow chains are required.

Conclusion

You've covered the essentials in this chapter. You know when to go, what documents to bring, how to budget for your journey, where to stay, and how to get to this amazing city.

As you progress through this book, you'll learn more about Trondheim, from its ancient sites to its wonderful cuisine and cultural events.

So, gather your belongings and prepare to go on an exciting journey to the Gateway to the North!

Chapter 3

TRONDHEIM EXPLORATION

Welcome to the epicentre of your Trondheim journey! In this chapter, we'll look at the city's highlights, from its lovely districts and renowned structures to its bustling cultural scene and outdoor activities.

Let us begin!

Neighborhoods and City Planning

Trondheim is a city that brilliantly blends a historic core with a modern flair. Its small size makes it ideal for walking, and you'll quickly notice the wonderful architecture that adorns the streets.

Let's take a look at the city's layout and neighborhoods:

Bakklandet: Bakklandet is one of my favorite neighborhoods, with beautiful wooden houses, cobblestone streets, and the historic Old Town Bridge (Gamle Bybro).

Take a walk down the Nidelva River and stop for a coffee at one of the riverfront cafes.

Midtbyen (City Center): This is the beating heart of Trondheim. Explore the lively streets filled with stores, restaurants, and historic structures.

Don't miss the majestic Nidaros Cathedral, a Gothic masterpiece and national treasure.

Solsiden: On the other side of the river is the stylish Solsiden area. This neighborhood is recognized for its modern waterfront architecture, restaurants, and bars, as well as its lively environment.

It's ideal for evening eating and nightlife.

Ilsvika: Head to Ilsvika along the Trondheimsfjord for a more relaxed experience. The neighborhood has beautiful promenades, beaches, and opportunities for a relaxed picnic with a view.

Landmarks and Attractions Not to Miss

Trondheim is overflowing with sights that will take your breath away. Here are a few that you should not miss:

Nidaros church: As I already stated, this magnificent church is the city's pride and joy. Its ornate facade and massive size are just amazing.

Don't forget to visit the adjacent Archbishop's Palace and gardens.

The Old Town Bridge (Gamle Bybro): This famous red bridge connects Bakklandet to the city center and is a must-see.

Just a short walk from here lies Kristiansten, a historic stronghold with panoramic views of the city.

Stiftsgrden: The largest wooden palace in Scandinavia, Stiftsgrden is a beautiful example of 18th-century Rococo architecture. The lovely gardens that surround it are equally appealing.

Ringve Museum: Music fans, this one is for you. The Ringve Museum houses a large collection of musical instruments from all around the world. The museum is located in a medieval manor with beautiful gardens.

Rockheim: If you like rock and pop music, this is the place to be. It is a modern museum that focuses on the history of Norwegian popular music and provides a hands-on, interactive experience.

Galleries and museums

The cultural landscape in Trondheim is robust, and you might spend days touring its museums and galleries. Here are a few more to consider:

Trondheim Art Museum: The Trondheim Art Museum houses a broad collection of Norwegian and international art, ranging from contemporary to classical. The museum's rotating displays ensure that there is always something new to view.

Sverresborg Trndelag Folk Museum: Visit this open-air museum to learn about the region's history. You can explore historic buildings, learn about traditional crafts, and get a feel for life in old Trndelag.

The Museum of Natural History and Archaeology is a must-see for nature lovers. It highlights the natural history of Norway, featuring unique exhibits on geology, paleontology, and archeology.

Galleri Ismene: For those interested in modern art, Galleri Ismene is a must-see. It exhibits works by local and international artists and serves as a focal point for the Trondheim art scene.

Parks and Outdoor Recreation

The natural surroundings of Trondheim give abundant chances for outdoor enthusiasts. Here are some ideas for enjoying the great outdoors:

Bymarka: This vast woodland area is at a short distance from the city center. In the winter, it's a refuge for hikers, mountain bikers, and cross-country skiers. Grkallen, be sure to trek to the overlook for a great view.

Trondheimsfjorden: The fjord offers a variety of water-based sports, including kayaking, sailing, and fishing. Explore the adjacent islands and take in the lovely coastline scenery.

Marinen and Munkholmen: Marinen is a beautiful fjordside park where you may relax, have a picnic, or take a picturesque stroll. You can take a boat from here to Munkholmen, a historic island with a former monastery and fortress.

Ladestien: This lovely coastline trail is ideal for a stroll or a bike ride. It meanders around the Trondheimsfjord, providing scenic vistas and excellent picnic places.

Trondheim Shopping

If you enjoy shopping, Trondheim has a diverse selection of worldwide brands, attractive boutiques, and local markets. Here are various retail districts to visit:

Nordre Gate: This is a shopping wonderland. There's a mix of high-end brands and independent stores here, as well as eateries for a brief shopping stop.

Merket: Merket is a shopping center with a variety of stores located in the middle of the city. It's ideal for shopping for souvenirs or the current fashion trends.

Sndre Gate: A pedestrian-friendly street filled with stores, restaurants, and cafes. It's a terrific place to go for a relaxed day of shopping.

Local Markets: If you're looking for locally produced goods, don't miss out on Trondheim's markets. Trondheim Torg is a lively market square filled with stores and stalls. Fresh food, homemade crafts, and other items are available.

Trondheim has something for everyone as you explore the city's neighborhoods, landmarks, cultural institutions, outdoor areas, and commercial districts.

You're bound to discover your own piece of Trondheim to enjoy, whether you're a history buff, an art lover, a nature enthusiast, or a shopaholic.

Stay tuned for more insights and recommendations to make your trip to Trondheim special!

Chapter 4

EXPERIENCING TRONDHEIM'S CULINARY DELIGHTS

Oh, the pleasure of discovering a new city's food culture! In this chapter, we'll take a deep dive into Trondheim's food culture. From traditional Norwegian cuisine to delectable seafood specialties to the best cafes, restaurants, and pubs, we'll take a culinary tour of the city. Let us begin!

Norwegian Cuisine at its Finest

Before we get into the specifics of where to eat in Trondheim, let's talk about the heart and soul of the city's food scene: traditional Norwegian cuisine.

The Norwegians have a strong connection to the land and the sea, and their cuisine reflects this:

Raspeballer: Raspeballer are potato dumplings that are popular in Norwegian cuisine. Raspeballer, served with a rich, delicious sauce and a side of meat, is a hearty comfort food you shouldn't miss.

Lutefisk: Lutefisk is a classic meal made from dried fish (typically cod) that has been rehydrated in a lye solution for the adventurous eater. It's frequently accompanied by bacon, peas, and a thick white sauce. Prepare yourself for an acquired taste!

Koldtbord: A Norwegian smorgasbord, Koldtbord consists of a variety of cold items such as fish, shellfish, salads, cold meats, and cheese. It's a fun way to try out different flavors.

Brunost: Also known as brown cheese, brunost has a sweet, caramel-like flavor that goes well with bread. It's one of those foods that you have to try to fully understand the Norwegian palate.

Seafood Specialties

Because of Trondheim's location along the Trondheimsfjord, fresh seafood is a must-try. Here are some seafood dishes that you should not miss:

Kongekrabbe (King Crab): A regional delicacy, king crab is usually served grilled, cooked, or in a creamy soup. The sweet and luscious meat is what seafood lovers crave.

Sjmat (Seafood Platter): Order a seafood platter for the ultimate seafood feast. It usually consists of shrimp, mussels, crab, and other local catches, served with bread and aioli.

Fiskesuppe (Fish Soup): A creamy fish soup containing a variety of seafood, vegetables, and seasonings. It's warm and cozy, making it ideal for chilly weather.

Restaurants, Cafes, and Bars

Now, let's look at where you can enjoy these Norwegian delicacies. Trondheim's gastronomic sector offers a broad selection of cafes, restaurants, and bars:

Cafes: Start your day the Norwegian way by visiting a nice café. Café 3B, Jacobsen & Svart, and Bakklandet Skydsstation are just a few of the city's beautiful coffee shops. Order a kanelbolle (cinnamon bun) and a cup of kaffe (coffee) and immerse yourself in the local culture.

Restaurants: If you're looking for a sit-down lunch, you're in luck. Nordst and Credo are two Michelin-starred Trondheim restaurants that serve exquisite, inventive dishes made using locally obtained ingredients.

Baklandet Skydsstation is a pleasant restaurant with a focus on local food that serves traditional Norwegian meals. Egon, a more casual eating experience with a mix of international and Norwegian dishes, is well worth a try.

Bars: Trondheim's nightlife is active, with a myriad of places to explore. From artisan beer bars like Café 3B to classic Norwegian pubs like Familien Bar, there's a wide range of places to taste the local brews and spirits.

Don't forget to try a Linie Aquavit, a caraway-flavored sea-aged spirit.

Markets and Street Food

Trondheim's street food and markets are good options for a more relaxed and budget-friendly dining experience. Here are a few must-see locations:

Mathallen Trondheim: This food hall is a gourmet treasure trove. Mathallen has everything for everyone's taste buds, from fresh fish to handmade cheese, international street food to Norwegian staples.

Trondheim Torg: Trondheim Torg is a lively marketplace in the city center where you may try local vegetables and street food.

It's a vibrant location to visit whether you're looking for a quick lunch or want to stock up on fresh supplies.

Fisherman's Wharf: There are seafood stalls along the Trondheimsfjord offering fresh catches of the day. It's the ideal location for a platter of shrimp or crab right on the water.

Dietary Options and Restrictions

Do you have dietary restrictions and want to travel? Not to worry, Trondheim is a culinary city that caters to a wide range of dietary requirements.

Many eateries provide vegetarian and vegan options, as well as gluten-free and lactose-free options. Simply inform your server of your dietary restrictions, and they will gladly accommodate you. Even traditional Norwegian cuisine can be altered to fit various diets.

Don't be afraid to ask locals for ideas while you explore Trondheim's culinary scene. They are always willing to recommend their favorite sites for traditional Norwegian fare, fresh fish, or a cup of coffee to warm your soul. You're guaranteed to experience a great gastronomic journey in Trondheim, a city that takes pride in its food culture.

Stay tuned for more excursions, including exploring the great outdoors and learning about the city's rich cultural past!

Chapter 5

PARTICIPATING IN LOCAL ACTIVITIES

Trondheim is more than just a tourist destination; it invites you to immerse yourself in the local culture.

In this chapter, we'll look at a variety of activities that will make your visit a memorable one, such as hiking through breathtaking natural landscapes, experiencing bustling nightlife, and indulging in moments of relaxation and wellness.

Hiking and Other outdoor Activities

Trondheim's proximity to breathtaking natural beauty is one of its most wonderful features. Forests, fjords, and mountains surround the city, providing outdoor enthusiasts with a playground of activities.

Here are a few outdoor activities you should not miss:

Bymarka: A big forested area just a short tram ride from the city center, Bymarka offers several routes for hiking, mountain biking, and cross-country skiing in the winter. The topography varies from deep woods to wide marshlands, making it a nature lover's ideal.

Grkallen: This notable Bymarka hill is famous for its panoramic views over Trondheim. Hike to the top for a panoramic view of the city, fjord, and surrounding countryside. It's also a great spot for a picnic.

Trondheimsfjorden: The Trondheimsfjord provides a variety of water-based sports, including kayaking, sailing, and fishing. Explore the adjacent islands, take in the peaceful coastline scenery, and, if you're lucky, spot some marine species.

Ladestien: This lovely seaside path along the Trondheimsfjord is ideal for a leisurely stroll or bike ride. It winds through beautiful scenery and has numerous excellent picnic places along the way.

Winter Recreation

Trondheim caters to people looking for winter adventures:

Skiing and Snowboarding: Skiing and snowboarding are available in the neighboring areas of Trondheim. For downhill action, head to resorts like Vassfjellet or Oppdal, or embrace cross-country skiing in the city's surrounding forests.

Ice Skating: During the winter, the city often installs ice skating rinks, such as the one at Trondheim Torg. It's a wonderful way to spend a cold winter day.

Northern Lights Chasing: While not guaranteed, you can sometimes see the spectacular Northern Lights close outside the city. Join a guided tour and cross your fingers for a glimpse of the aurora borealis.

Festivals and Special Events

The cultural calendar in Trondheim is jam-packed with intriguing festivals and events. Here are a few to consider when planning your visit:

Olavsfestdagene: Held in late July each year, this festival honors the city's patron saint, Olav Tryggvason, with a variety of cultural events, music performances, and historical reenactments.

Trondheim Jazz Festival: Jazz fans, take note of the Trondheim Jazz Festival! This May festival features an amazing array of foreign and Norwegian jazz artists.

Trondheim Calling: Held in February, Trondheim Calling is a music event that connects listeners to upcoming musicians from Norway and abroad. It's an incredible chance to discover new tunes and talents.

Midt-Norsk Matfestival: This is a must-see event for foodies. It's a celebration of regional culinary traditions in September, featuring food stalls, tastings, and cooking demonstrations.

Entertainment and Nightlife

Trondheim's nightlife is bustling, with numerous possibilities for evening entertainment. Here are a few highlights:

Familien Bar: This iconic bar features live music, DJs, and a laid-back environment. It's a nice place to have a drink and meet the locals.

Kultursenteret ISAK: ISAK is a city cultural center that conducts a variety of activities, from concerts and art exhibitions to workshops and film screenings. Check out their schedule for the most up-to-date information.

Studentersamfundet: If you're in town for a concert or event, get a ticket to Studentersamfundet.

This legendary student organization produces performances and gatherings that attract both students and locals.

Wellness and relaxation

After all of the excitement, a little downtime is in order. Here are some places to unwind and discover your Zen:

SALTEN Kurbad & Spa:

SALTEN, located in the city center, provides a variety of wellness services, including saunas and hot tubs, as well as massage and spa treatments. It's the ideal spot to unwind.

Parks and Green Spaces:

Trondheim is home to several magnificent parks, like Munkholmen and Marinen, where you may take a leisurely stroll, have a picnic, or simply rest in a scenic setting.

Yoga and Wellness Centers:

Look for yoga studios and wellness centers that offer classes and services to assist you in finding your inner balance.

Participating in local activities in Trondheim is all about embracing the city's lifestyle, from enjoying the wonderful outdoors to attending cultural events and relaxing. With this guide on your side, your trip around Trondheim will be a memorable blend of adventure, culture, and relaxation.

Stay tuned for further insights and pointers on how to make the most of your vacation to this stunning Norwegian city!

Chapter 6

GETTING AROUND TRONDHEIM

Now that you've seen Trondheim's beauties, it's time to learn how to move around this attractive Norwegian city. I'll walk you through the options for getting from one experience to the next, from efficient public transportation to cycling, taxis, and auto rentals.

Public Transportation

Trondheim has a well-organized public transportation infrastructure that makes getting around the city and its neighboring areas easy. Here's a rundown of what you should know:

Trams and Buses: Trondheim's tram and bus network is vast and dependable. The city core, suburbs, and adjacent attractions are all easily accessible. Buses are well-known for their punctuality and comfort, while trams provide an enjoyable way to see the city.

Tickets and Fares: Generally, tickets are good for both trams and buses. If you plan to take public transit frequently, you can buy single-ride tickets or save money by purchasing a day pass. Check the local transit authority's website or app for the most up-to-date ticket prices and schedules.

Travel Cards: For longer visits, consider purchasing a travel card, such as the AtB Card, which may be pre-loaded with credit for hassle-free travel. It's a practical and cost-effective alternative.

Renting a Vehicle

Renting a car in Trondheim is a reasonable choice if you want the flexibility of having your own wheels. Here are some things to bear in mind:

Renting an Automobile: There are numerous automobile rental firms in the city as well as at Trondheim Airport Vaernes. Vehicles ranging from compact automobiles to larger SUVs are available. To get the greatest rates and availability, book your rental in advance.

Driving in Trondheim: Trondheim's road network is well-maintained, making exploring the city and its surrounds a snap. Remember to drive on the right side of the road in Norway, and seat belts are required for all passengers.

Parking: While parking in the outskirts is normally easy, it can be more difficult in the city center. Prepare for parking expenses and use parking garages if needed. Take note that Trondheim has a low-emission zone with restricted access for certain vehicles.

Bike Riding in Trondheim

Trondheim is a bike-friendly city, with designated bike lanes and routes that make exploring on two wheels a pleasure. Here are some pointers for getting around by bike:

City Bikes: Trondheim Bysykkel, Trondheim's bike-sharing system, is available. You can borrow a bike for short trips and return it at one of the city's bike stations.

It's a convenient and environmentally beneficial mode of transportation.

Bike Rentals: If you want a more personal cycling experience, there are various bike rental businesses throughout the city that can equip you with a quality bike for the duration of your stay.

Biking Infrastructure: Trondheim is well-known for its cycling infrastructure, which includes well-marked bike lanes and pathways. This makes biking throughout the city and its attractive surrounds, such as Bymarka, easy and safe.

Taxis and Ride-Sharing Services

Taxis are accessible in Trondheim, however they are often more expensive than other modes of transportation. If you require a taxi, you may either hail one on the street or reserve one through a taxi app.

Uber and other ridesharing services are also available and can be a convenient option.

Accessibility in Trondheim

Trondheim is dedicated to accessibility and provides a variety of services and facilities for visitors with special needs. Consider the following:

Public Transportation: Ramps and dedicated areas are available on trams and buses for passengers with mobility issues. The tram stops and bus stations in the city are wheelchair accessible.

Wheelchair Rentals: If you require a wheelchair or mobility scooter during your visit, Trondheim has rental services available.

Accessible Attractions: Many of Trondheim's renowned sights, such as the Nidaros Cathedral and museums, are accessible to visitors with impairments. If you have any specific concerns or questions, please contact the venues ahead of time for information and support.

Trondheim's commitment to accessibility and efficient public transit makes it a welcome city for all visitors.

Whether you're exploring the city on foot, by bike, or by public transportation, you'll find it easy to get around.

With these options you can embark on new adventures, discover hidden treasures, and make the most of your vacation to this great Norwegian city.

Chapter 7

DAY TRIPS AND EXCURSIONS

While Trondheim itself is an intriguing location, its environs provide a plethora of day trip options. In this chapter, we'll leave the city to see coastal villages, stunning fjords, learn about history and culture, and even go on daring wildlife excursions.

Let us embark on an adventure!

Tours of Coastal Villages and Fjords

The Trndelag region has a beautiful coastline and attractive settlements within a short drive or boat trip from Trondheim. Consider the following coastal jewels and fjord tours:

Røros: Rros is a picturesque mining village with well-preserved wooden structures that is a UNESCO World Heritage site.

It is a three-hour journey from Trondheim and is noted for its history and distinct atmosphere.

Hitra and Frya: These two islands are ideal for a relaxing coastal getaway. You may go fishing, explore the gorgeous coastal sceneries, or simply relax by the sea. Ferries run on a regular basis from Trondheim to these islands.

Fjord Tours: Trondheim's location on the Trondheimsfjord provides for breathtaking fjord trips. Cruises can transport you through the stunning landscapes and attractive fjord communities such as Stjrdal and Orkanger, among others.

Trondheim's Surrounding Natural Beauty

The natural splendor surrounding Trondheim is simply breathtaking. If you enjoy nature, these day outings are a must:

Bymarka: Only a short tram ride away, Bymarka is a hiking and outdoor enthusiast's paradise. Explore the woodland, hike to Grkallen, or stroll along Ladestien along the fjord.

Fosen Peninsula: The Fosen Peninsula, located just across the fjord from Trondheim, provides a plethora of outdoor sports. Hike up Stokkheia's mountain for panoramic views, try kayaking, or visit the quaint village of fjord.

Munkholmen: This historic island is only a short boat journey from Trondheim and provides an insight into Norwegian history. Visit the historic monastery and fortress, have a picnic, or simply relax and enjoy the tranquil surroundings.

Historical and Cultural Day Trips

If you're a history or culture geek, there are lots of day trip choices to suit your interests:

Stiklestad: Travel back in time with a visit to Stiklestad, the site of the Battle of Stiklestad in 1030. This historical landmark is around a 2-hour drive from Trondheim and features an interactive museum as well as open-air entertainment.

Copper Mining at Lkken Verk: Visit Lkken Verk to learn about Norway's industrial legacy. The old mining town is about a 2-hour drive from Trondheim and has a rich history as well as well-preserved buildings.

Falstad Center: A visit to the Falstad Center will provide you with a better understanding of Norway's history during WWII. It's a 1.5-hour trip from Trondheim and is a former prison camp that now houses a museum and educational center.

Adventure and Wildlife Excursions

If you're looking for adventure and wildlife encounters, these day outings will not disappoint:

Whale Watching in Trndelag: The Trndelag coast is recognized for its abundance of marine life. From Trondheim, take a boat cruise to see whales, seals, and other sea creatures in their natural habitat.

River Rafting in Stjrdal: The Stjrdal River offers thrilling river rafting activities within a short drive from Trondheim. It's a great way to get your adrenaline going.

Winter Sports in Oppdal: In the winter, the ski resort in Oppdal is a winter sports enthusiast's heaven. It's about a 2-hour drive from Trondheim and offers skiing, snowboarding, and other winter activities.

Planning Your Day Trips

When organizing day trips from Trondheim, keep the following points in mind:

Transport: Depending on your destination, you may require a car, a ferry, or a guided tour. Make sure you've planned ahead of time for the essential transportation.

Timing: Consider the time it takes to get to your day trip location as well as the amount of time you want to spend there. Some areas may require an entire day to explore, while others can be done in a matter of hours.

Weather: Be aware of the weather and any seasonal factors. Winter day trips, for example, are ideal for snow sports, whilst summer may be preferable for beach experiences.

Local Information: Make sure to verify local information as well as any specific guidelines or regulations for the sites you intend to visit. It is best to book wildlife trips through reliable travel operators.

Trondheim is a fantastic base for experiencing the Trndelag region's rich beauty, history, culture, and adventure, with so many wonderful day trip possibilities at your fingertips.

These day trips will add rich layers to your Trondheim adventure, whether you're searching for a calm coastal vacation, a deep dive into history, or a thrilling animal encounter.

Chapter 8

INTERACTING WITH LOCALS

One of the most enjoyable aspects of our travels as tourists is the connections we build with locals. In Trondheim, you'll find warm and welcoming Norwegians ready to share their culture and way of life.

This chapter is all about social etiquette, making friends, responsible travel, being safe, and being prepared for any emergency while experiencing this wonderful Norwegian city.

Social Protocol and Customs

Understanding local customs and social etiquette is the first step toward building lasting relationships with Trondheim people. Here are some things to bear in mind:

Punctuality is important to the Norwegians. It is considered a sign of respect to arrive on time for appointments, meetings, or dinner reservations.

Norwegians appreciate their personal space. When conversing with others, it's necessary to keep a comfortable physical distance, and it's not typical to engage in lengthy physical contact, such as hugging or kissing, when you first meet.

While service costs are frequently included in restaurant bills, it is generally customary to give a little tip. Most people like it when you round up the amount or leave a 5-10% tip. Tipping taxi drivers and service personnel is also customary.

Small Talk: Norwegians may appear quiet at first, but if you engage in conversation, you'll find them warm and pleasant. Weather, wildlife, and mutual hobbies are excellent conversation starters.

Friendship in Trondheim

Trondheim is a wonderful spot to meet locals and fellow travelers and make new acquaintances. Here are several ways to interact with others:

Participate in Local Activities: Attend local events, workshops, or classes. These activities, whether a cooking class, a hiking group, or a cultural festival, are ideal for meeting locals who share your interests.

Volunteering: Volunteering is an excellent way to give back to the community while also connecting with people who are enthusiastic about the same causes. During your visit, look for local volunteer opportunities.

Cafes and Bars: Trondheim's cafes and bars offer a casual setting for mingling. Start a conversation with the individual next to you or ask the barista for recommendations on local hotspots.

Language Exchange: Language exchange events are a fun ways to practice and connect with native speakers if you're interested in learning the local language.

Sustainable and Responsible Tourism

Responsible tourism is crucial in Trondheim, as it is anywhere else. Here are some tips for being a responsible traveler:

Reduce Your Environmental Impact: Follow local garbage disposal and recycling guidelines. Bring a reusable water bottle and shopping bag to reduce your usage of single-use plastic.

Support Local Businesses: Choose locally owned shops, restaurants, and lodging to support local businesses. Your purchases benefit the local economy and provide a more authentic experience.

Respect Nature: Stay on authorized trails, practice the Leave No Trace principles, and show respect for wildlife and nature when enjoying the magnificent Norwegian outdoors.

Learn About Sustainable Practices: Trondheim has a strong commitment to sustainability. Visit eco-friendly companies and talk to residents about their efforts to safeguard the environment.

How to Stay Safe in Trondheim

Trondheim is a relatively safe city, however it's always a good idea to be cautious and observant. Here are some safety precautions:

Street Safety: Trondheim's streets are safe to stroll on, even at night. However, keep an eye on your stuff and avoid poorly lit or deserted areas.

Traffic & Transportation: Use caution when crossing roadways and follow traffic laws. Public transit is safe and dependable.

Natural Hazards: If you intend to explore the surrounding nature, be mindful of weather conditions, dress appropriately, and be ready for rapid changes in weather.

Emergency Services: For all emergencies, including police, fire, and medical aid, dial 112 in Norway.

Emergency Information

While it is unlikely that you will experience any emergencies during your stay to Trondheim, it is essential that you are prepared. Here is some critical emergency information:

Emergency Number: In Norway, the emergency services number is 112. For police, fire, ambulance, and other emergencies, dial this number.

Medical Care: Trondheim has first-rate medical facilities. The St. Olav's Hospital (St. Olavs Hospital) is the city's primarily hospital, providing emergency medical services. They have a dedicated emergency unit.

Embassy and Consulate: Depending on your nationality, your Norwegian embassy or consulate can assist you with a misplaced passport, legal concerns, or other situations. It's a good idea to know the address and phone number of your embassy or consulate ahead of time.

Exploring Trondheim and meeting its friendly residents is a lovely experience.

You'll have the opportunity to create lasting memories and unforgettable moments in this enchanting Norwegian city by respecting local customs and etiquette, building friendships, being a responsible traveler, and being safe.

Have a wonderful trip in Trondheim, and may your interactions with locals be full with warmth and cultural interchange!

Chapter 9

TRAVEL RESOURCES

As we continue our exploration of Trondheim, it's critical to understand where to discover valuable resources that can make your stay more comfortable, secure, and pleasurable.

In this chapter, I'll walk you through important travel resources such as tourist information centers, embassies and consulates, staying connected to the internet, managing your funds, and the value of travel insurance.

Tourist Information Centers

When it comes to exploring a new place, tourist information centers are your best friend. They give maps, brochures, and helpful assistance in Trondheim. Here are some important centers to be aware of:

Visit Trondheim Tourist Information: Located in the heart of the city at Nordre gate 11, Visit Trondheim gives a wealth of information on local attractions, activities, and more. The staff is quite educated and can assist you in planning your days in the city.

Trondheim Airport Vaernes Tourist Information: If you arrive by plane, you can get a head start on your

Trondheim experience at the airport's tourist information office. It's in the Arrivals Hall, and the helpful personnel can provide maps and directions.

Online Resources: Before you even arrive in Trondheim, check out their official tourism website. It's jam-packed with information about lodging, activities, events, and much more.

Consulates and Embassies

While we hope your trip to Trondheim goes smoothly, it's always a good idea to know the location of your country's embassy or consulate in case you run into any problems. Here are some of the more important ones in Trondheim:

Embassy of the United States: The United States Embassy in Oslo is the country's major diplomatic mission and is located in the capital city. If you are a US citizen, this is the place to go for any consular help.

United Kingdom Embassy: The British Embassy is also located in Oslo. You can contact them for consular services, and they will help you in an emergency.

Consulates: Various nations have consulates in Trondheim, which are often in charge of more specialized services. Your country's embassy or official government website will provide a list of consulates in Trondheim as well as contact information.

Communication and the Internet

Staying connected when traveling is vital, and Trondheim makes it easy. Here are some suggestions for staying in touch:

Mobile Network: Norway has a dependable mobile network. You may get a local SIM card at Trondheim

Airport or any of the city's mobile service providers. It's a cheap method to get internet access during your stay.

Wi-Fi: Wi-Fi is available in most hotels, cafes, restaurants, and public areas in Trondheim. When you need to search up information or share your adventures with friends and family, you'll have no issue remaining connected.

Language: While most Norwegians speak English efficiently, knowing some basic Norwegian words is useful for effective conversation. A simple "hello" (hei) and "thank you" (takk) can help you connect with the people.

Money Matters

Managing your finances during your Trondheim visit is easy, but it's always a good idea to plan ahead of time. Here's what you should know:

Currency: The Norwegian Krone (NOK) is the currency in Trondheim, as it is across Norway. Before you travel, make sure to check the current currency rate.

ATMs: ATMs are widely distributed throughout Trondheim (known as minibanks in Norwegian). You can use your credit or debit card to withdraw local money. Simply inquire with your bank regarding overseas transaction fees.

Credit Cards: Visa and Mastercard are the most generally accepted credit cards in Trondheim. It's a good idea to keep some cash on hand for little purchases, but cards are sufficient for most transactions.

Tipping: Tipping is not required in Trondheim, but it is common to round up your total or leave a 5-10% tip in restaurants and cafes if service is not included. Tipping taxi drivers and service personnel is also customary.

Travel Insurance

Travel insurance may not be the most thrilling subject, but it is an essential component of any trip to ensure peace of mind. Here are a few reasons why you ought to consider about it:

Medical Protection: Travel insurance can give financial protection in the event of a medical emergency, which can be costly when traveling overseas.

Trip Cancellation: If you have to cancel your trip due to unforeseen circumstances, travel insurance can help you recoup your expenses.

Lost or Stolen Belongings: Insurance can cover the replacement or compensation of lost or stolen belongings such as passports, luggage, or precious devices.

Peace of Mind: Travel insurance can act as a safety net in the event of an unexpected event, such as a flight delay or natural disaster.

Before choosing a travel insurance plan, thoroughly read the terms and conditions, understand what is covered, and evaluate your unique needs for your Trondheim vacation.

You're now well-prepared to explore Trondheim with confidence, having gone through vital travel resources for your trip. These services ensure that your journey is smooth, pleasurable, and safe, whether you require local information, assistance from your embassy or consulate, dependable communication choices, financial management, or travel insurance.

Enjoy every minute of your time in Trondheim and relish the unforgettable experiences that this magnificent city has to offer!

Chapter 10

APPENDIX

As we near the end of our tour of Trondheim, I'd would like to give you some useful tools and resources to make your stay even more enjoyable.

Sample itineraries for your Trondheim excursion, a complete packing list to ensure you're prepared, handy Norwegian words to help you engage with locals, and a list of supplementary reading and references for further research are all included in this appendix.

Sample Itineraries

Here are three sample itineraries to help you make the most of your time in Trondheim, each catering to different interests and durations:

Cultural Immersion (3 Days):

Learn about the city's fascinating history and culture. Visit the Archbishop's Palace, Nidaros Cathedral, and the Ringve Music Museum.

Take a walk through Bakklandet and a fjord tour for amazing views. At local restaurants, try traditional Norwegian cuisine.

Nature and Adventure (4 Days):

Immerse yourself in the natural splendor of Trondheim. Hike in Bymarka in the summer, ski in the winter, and kayak in the fjords in the summer.

For coastal experiences, take a day trip to Roros and another to Hitra and Frya.

Family-Friendly (5 Days):

Plan a trip that is suitable for all ages. Explore the Science Center, spend a day at the Kristiansten Fortress, and spend a day relaxing in the gorgeous parks.

Don't forget to try some Norwegian meals that are suitable for children.

Packing List for Trondheim

Packing for Trondheim can be easy if you're prepared for changing weather conditions. Here's a packing list to make sure you have everything:

Weather-appropriate Clothing: Layer up for Trondheim's unpredictable weather. A waterproof jacket, strong walking shoes, and a good umbrella are all required.

Adapters and Converters: Norway utilizes Type C and F power sockets, so carry the necessary adapters and converters with you.

While most Norwegians speak English, having a Norwegian phrasebook can be extremely useful and appreciated by locals.

Reusable Water Bottle: Carrying a reusable water bottle might help you save money and minimize plastic waste. Trondheim's tap water is of high quality and safe to drink.

Prescriptions and First-Aid Kit: Bring any prescription medications you may need, as well as a small first-aid kit for minor injuries.

Guidebook or Maps: A guidebook or maps can be extremely useful for navigating the city and planning your daily travels.

Useful Norwegian Expressions

While many Norwegians understand English, learning a few simple Norwegian words can enrich your trip and show respect for the local culture. Here are some sentences to help you get started:

- Hello - Hei
- Please - Vaer så snill
- Thank you - Takk
- Yes - Ja
- No - Nei
- Excuse me - Unnskyld meg
- Good morning - God morgen
- Good afternoon - God ettermiddag
- Good evening - God kveld

- Goodbye - Ha det
- I don't understand - Jeg forstår ikke

Additional Reading and References

If you want to learn more about Trondheim's history, culture, and attractions, look into the following books, websites, and references:

Books:

"Trondheim: En Byhistorie" by Egil Remi Hagen

"Insight Guides Norway" by Insight Guides

Websites:

Visit Trondheim (https://www.visittrondheim.no/)

Trondheim Municipality Official Website (https://www.trondheim.kommune.no/)

Local Publications:

Local newspapers and publications in Trondheim often cover current events, restaurant reviews, and insider information. Check out "Adressa" and "Trd.by" for the most recent updates.

Online Discussion Boards:

Websites such as TripAdvisor provide travelers with information, guidance, and suggestions.

Official Government Websites:

Consider visiting your government's official travel advisory website for information on travel regulations and safety.

With these tools, you'll be well-equipped to immerse yourself in the magic of Trondheim and its culture and history.

These resources will be essential companions on your travel, whether you're interested in learning more about the city, planning your vacation, or understanding local customs.

Have a wonderful stay in Trondheim, and may your adventures be filled with wonder and excitement!

Printed in Great Britain
by Amazon